GREAT WHITE SHARK
(CARCHARODON CARCHARIAS)

SIZE:
12 to 16 feet (3.7 to 4.9 m) long

ON THE MENU:
Fish, rays, other sharks, sea lions, seals, dolphins, otters,
sea turtles, and carrion

WHERE IN THE WORLD:
Temperate waters around the world; large great whites have
been found in tropical waters as well

CHECK IT OUT!
Great white sharks are viviparous. This means that the eggs hatch inside
the mother's body, and the mother gives birth to live young.

WHERE IN THE WORLD

GREAT WHITE SHARK
A QUICK GETAWAY

Baby great white sharks (called pups) are about 5 feet (1.5 m) long when they're born. After birth, the pup immediately swims away from its mother. Why? The mother likely sees the baby as prey!

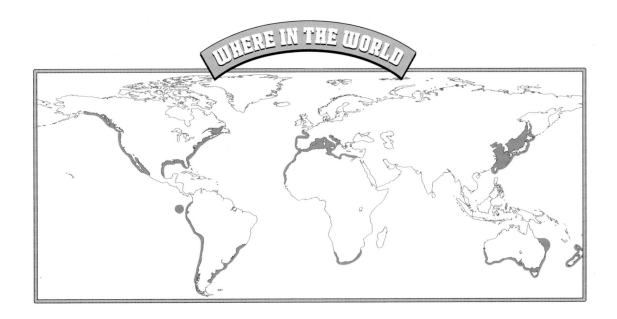

WHERE IN THE WORLD

GREAT WHITE SHARK

CHOMP!

Great white sharks are skilled predators. Their mouths are lined with up to 300 serrated, triangular teeth arranged in rows. When great whites attack their prey, they don't chew; they bite off large chunks of meat and swallow it whole.

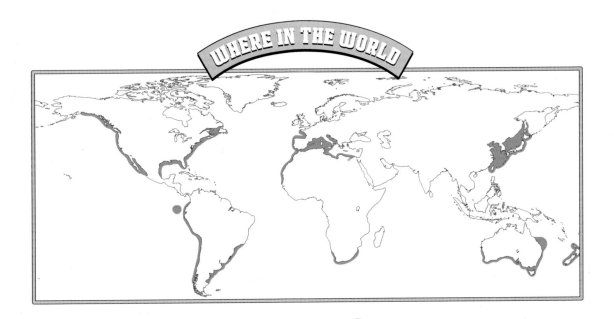

WHERE IN THE WORLD

OCEANIC WHITETIP SHARK
(CARCHARHINUS LONGIMANUS)

SIZE:
On average, 6 feet (1.8 m) long; can grow to be 13 feet (4 m) long

ON THE MENU:
Bony fishes, such as lancetfish, barracuda, dolphinfish, marlin, tuna, and mackerels; also stingrays, sea turtles, sea birds, squid, crustaceans, and carrion

WHERE IN THE WORLD:
Tropical and subtropical waters around the world

CHECK IT OUT!
Whitetip sharks have been observed swimming with shortfin pilot whales. Scientists believe the sharks accompany the whales because the whales are skilled at locating squid, one of the sharks' favorite foods.

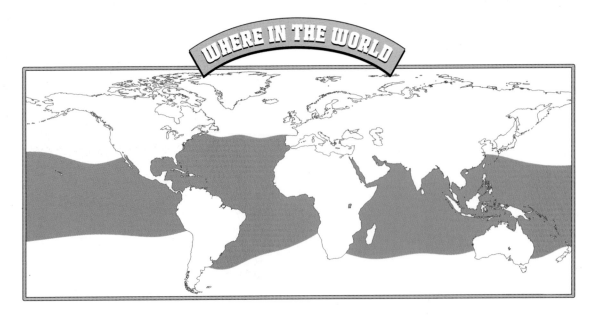

WHERE IN THE WORLD

OCEANIC BLACKTIP SHARK
(CARCHARHINUS LIMBATUS)

SIZE:
5 feet (1.5 m) long on average, can grow to be 8 feet (2.4 m) long;
average 40 lbs. (18 kg)

ON THE MENU:
Herring, sardines, anchovies, crustaceans, squid, catfish, grouper, flatfish,
porcupine fish, dogfish, sharpnose sharks, skates, and stingrays

WHERE IN THE WORLD:
Coastal, tropical, subtropical, coastal shelf, and island waters around the world

CHECK IT OUT!
Blacktip sharks charge vertically toward the surface of the water to attack
schools of fish swimming at the surface. The sharks move so quickly that they
breach out of the water, sometimes spinning around three or four times!

WHERE IN THE WORLD

BLUE SHARK
(PRIONACE GLAUCA)

SIZE:
6 to 10½ feet (1.8 to 3.2 m) long; can grow to be 12½ feet (3.8 m) long

ON THE MENU:
Squid, cuttlefish, octopus, and bony fishes; will also eat marine mammal carrion

WHERE IN THE WORLD:
Tropical and temperate waters around the world

CHECK IT OUT!
Blue sharks are dangerous to humans!
They have been known to circle swimmers or divers for 15 minutes or more, most likely in an attempt to figure out whether to attack.

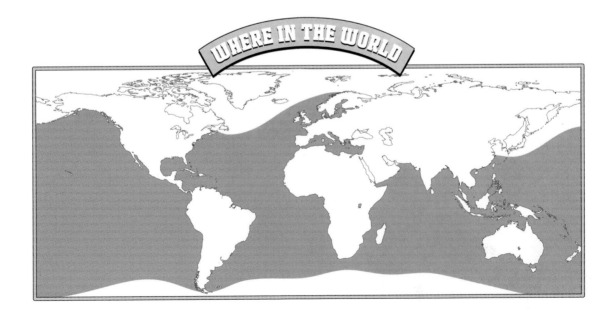

WHERE IN THE WORLD

LEMON SHARK
(NEGAPRION BREVIROSTRIS)

SIZE:
8 to 10 feet (2.4 to 3 m) long

ON THE MENU:
Catfish, porcupine fish, cowfish, guitarfish, stingrays, eagle rays, crabs, crayfish, sea birds, and smaller sharks

WHERE IN THE WORLD:
East Coast of the United States to southern Brazil; Gulf of Mexico and the Caribbean; Senegal and the Ivory Coast of Africa; Gulf of California south to Ecuador

CHECK IT OUT!
Female lemon sharks give birth to pups in shallow water. After birth, the pups remain in these nursery grounds for several years.

WHERE IN THE WORLD

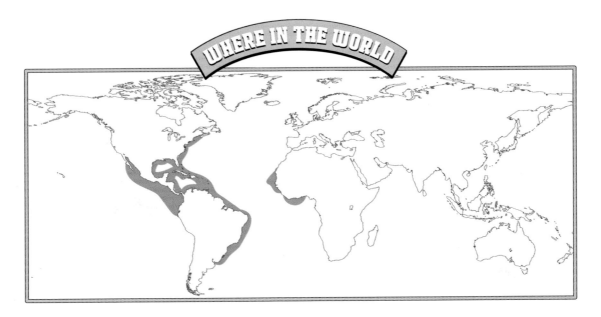

BLACKTIP REEF SHARK
(CARCHARHINUS MELANOPTERUS)

SIZE:
6 feet (1.6 m) long

ON THE MENU:
Reef fish, such as sturgeon and mullet

WHERE IN THE WORLD:
Coral reefs and shallow lagoons in the tropical Indian and Pacific Oceans;
also the Mediterranean Sea

CHECK IT OUT!
Blacktip reef sharks have 23-28 finely serrated teeth in their
upper jaw and 21-27 in the lower jaw.

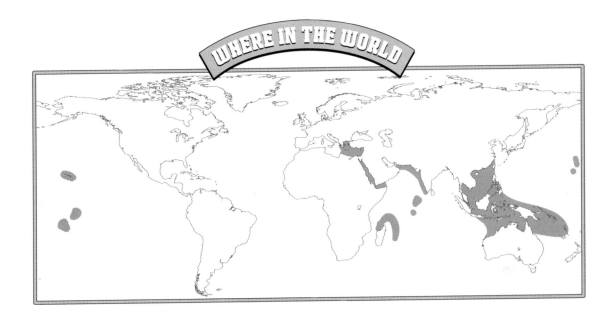

WHERE IN THE WORLD

BLACKTIP REEF SHARK

SAVE THE SHARKS!

The blacktip reef shark is considered "Near Threatened" by the World Conservation Union (IUCN). They get caught in fishing nets intended for other fish. These sharks have been known to occasionally bite people who are swimming or wading, but they are not a serious threat to humans.

WHERE IN THE WORLD

WHITETIP REEF SHARK
(TRIAENODON OBESUS)

SIZE:
About 5½ feet (1.7 m) long

ON THE MENU:
Octopus, lobsters, crabs, and bony fishes, such as eels, snappers, and parrotfishes

WHERE IN THE WORLD:
Red Sea, Indian Ocean, and central and eastern Pacific Ocean

CHECK IT OUT!
Whitetip reef sharks are most active at night. During the daytime, groups of these sharks gather in caves and remain motionless for long periods of time, stacked on top of each other like a pile of firewood.

WHERE IN THE WORLD

SHORTFIN MAKO SHARK
(ISURUS OXYRINCHUS)

SIZE:
5-8 feet (1.5-2.5 m) long; about 1,000 lbs. (450 kg)

ON THE MENU:
Tuna, herring, mackerel, swordfish, and porpoise

WHERE IN THE WORLD:
Temperate and tropical oceans around the world

CHECK IT OUT!
Shortfin makos are fast sharks. They can reach speeds of up to 20 mph (32 kph) and even leap out of the water!

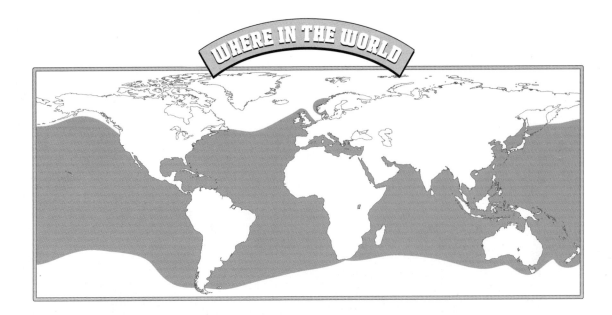

WHERE IN THE WORLD

SHORTFIN MAKO SHARK
SAVE THE SHARKS!

The World Conservation Union (IUCN) has listed the shortfin mako shark as "Near Threatened" because their populations have decreased sharply in recent years. Shortfin makos are caught and killed worldwide for their meat. They also get trapped in tuna and swordfish nets.

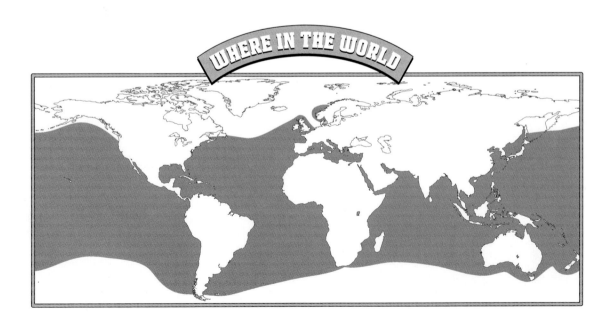

WHERE IN THE WORLD

BULL SHARK
(CARCHARHINUS LEUCAS)

SIZE:
7 to 11½ feet (2.1 to 3.5 m) long; 200 to 500 lbs. (90 to 230 kg)

ON THE MENU:
Fish (including other sharks and rays); dolphins, turtles, birds, mollusks, and crustaceans

WHERE IN THE WORLD:
Coastal tropical and subtropical waters around the world; also found in a few freshwater lakes and rivers

CHECK IT OUT!
Many shark experts consider the bull shark to be the most dangerous shark to humans. These large sharks are found in areas in the tropics that are frequented by many people.

WHERE IN THE WORLD

HAMMERHEAD SHARK
(SPHYRNA MOKARRAN)

SIZE:
Average 11½ feet (3.5 m) long; average 500 lbs. (230 kg)

ON THE MENU:
Stingrays (even the tail spine!), crabs, squid, octopus, lobsters, grouper, catfish, and flatfishes

WHERE IN THE WORLD:
Coastal tropical and subtropical waters around the world

CHECK IT OUT!
There are four types of hammerhead shark: the smooth hammerhead, scalloped hammerhead, great hammerhead, and the bonnethead.

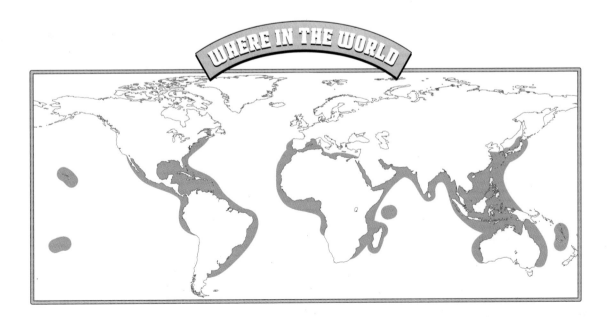

HAMMERHEAD SHARK

SAVE THE SHARKS!

The great hammerhead shark is considered "Endangered"
by the World Conservation Union (IUCN), even though scientists
do not have specific numbers on the shark's population.
Great hammerheads get caught in fishing nets intended for
other types of fish. As with just about all species of sharks,
it's believed that without conservation protection, great hammerheads
will continue to decline.

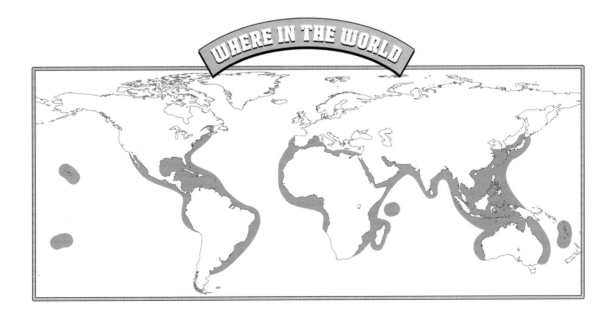

WHERE IN THE WORLD

THRESHER SHARK
(ALOPIAS VULPINUS)

SIZE:
16½ to 20 feet (5 to 6 m) long

ON THE MENU:
Squid; bony fish, such as herring, mackerel, bluefish, and butterfish

WHERE IN THE WORLD:
Tropical and temperate waters around the world

CHECK IT OUT!
Thresher sharks are considered harmless to humans. They are shy and not easily approachable, but they have been known to attack boats.

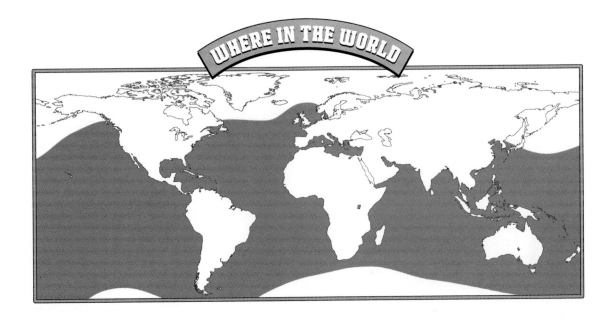

COMMON SAWSHARK
(PRISTIPHORUS CIRRATUS)

SIZE:
About 5 feet (1.5 m) long

ON THE MENU:
Small fish, crustaceans, and squid

WHERE IN THE WORLD:
Southern coast of Australia

CHECK IT OUT!
Common sawsharks are born with their teeth folded back, most likely to prevent injury to the mother during birth. The teeth straighten soon after the sharks are born.

WHERE IN THE WORLD

SAND TIGER SHARK
(CARCHARIAS TAURUS)

SIZE:
4 to 10½ feet (1.2 to 3.2 m)

ON THE MENU:
Herring, bluefish, eels, snappers, remoras, sea bass, rays, squid, crabs, lobsters, and smaller sharks

WHERE IN THE WORLD:
Warm coastal waters around the world, except for the eastern Pacific Ocean

CHECK IT OUT!
Sand tiger sharks come to the surface of the water and take in large gulps of air. This allows them to hover in the water without moving as they scope out their prey.

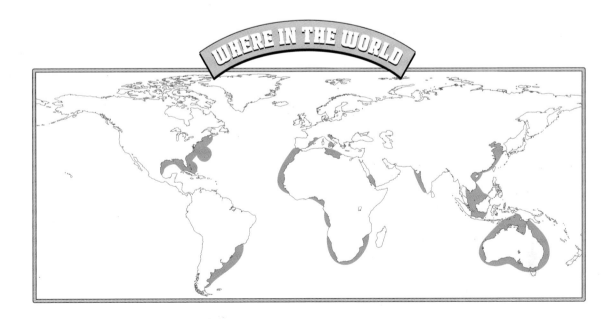

SAND TIGER SHARK
CHOMP!

Sand tiger sharks are big eaters. They feed at night, usually staying close to the bottom. Sometimes they hunt in groups and may attack fishing nets full of fish.

WHERE IN THE WORLD

TIGER SHARK
(GALEOCERDO CUVIER)

SIZE:
10 to 14 feet (3 to 4.3 m) long; can weigh more than 850 to 1,400 lbs. (385 to 635 kg)

ON THE MENU:
Sea turtles, rays, other sharks, bony fishes, sea birds, dolphins, squid, crustaceans, and carrion

WHERE IN THE WORLD:
Tropical and temperate waters around the world, except in the Mediterranean Sea

CHECK IT OUT!
Tiger sharks will eat just about anything!
One female tiger shark that was caught in the Red Sea had two empty cans, a plastic bottle, burlap sacks, a squid, and a large fish in her stomach.

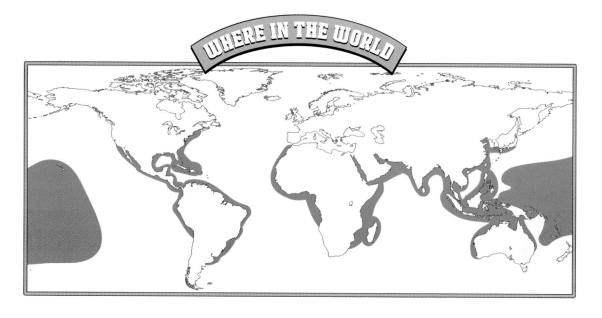

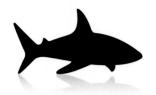

LEOPARD SHARK
(TRIAKIS SEMIFASCIATA)

SIZE:
5 to 6 feet (1.5 to 1.8 m) long; up to 42 lbs. (19 kg)

ON THE MENU:
Crabs, shrimp, clams, octopus, bony fish, rays, and fish eggs

WHERE IN THE WORLD:
Eastern Pacific Ocean from Oregon to the Gulf of Mexico

CHECK IT OUT!
Leopard sharks mutilate their prey! They have been known to eat only part of the animal, leaving behind the rest of their meal.

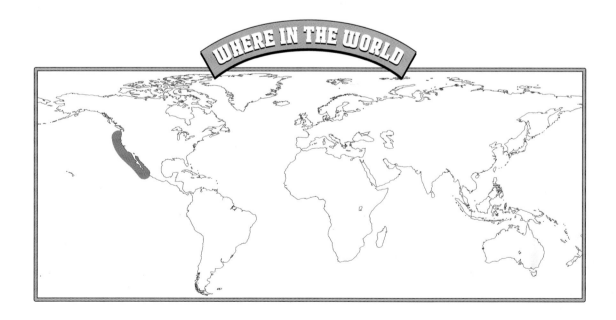

WHERE IN THE WORLD

WHALE SHARK
(RHINCODON TYPUS)

SIZE:
25 feet (7.6 m) long on average; can grow to be 46 feet (14 m) long

ON THE MENU:
Plankton, crustaceans, krill, small fish, and squid

WHERE IN THE WORLD:
Tropical and warm temperate seas around the world, except in the Mediterranean

CHECK IT OUT!
Unlike the basking shark, which swims forward to take in and filter water, the whale shark sucks in the water. It then filters out the tiny animals for its meal.

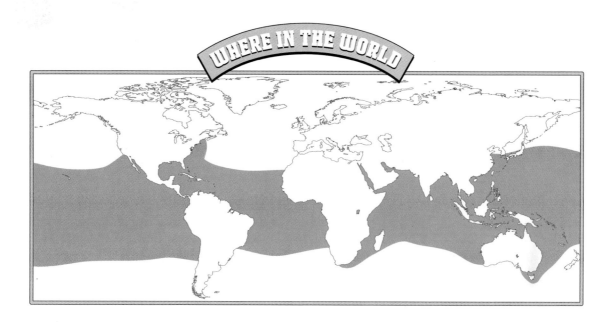

WHERE IN THE WORLD

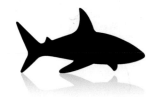

BASKING SHARK
(CETORHINUS MAXIMUS)

SIZE:
30 to 40 feet (9 to 12 m) long; weighs up to 4 tons (4 tonnes)

ON THE MENU:
Small crustaceans, invertebrate larvae, baby fish, and fish eggs

WHERE IN THE WORLD:
Arctic and temperate waters around the world

CHECK IT OUT!
Basking sharks swim with their mouths wide open, taking in and filtering around 2,000 tons of water every hour.

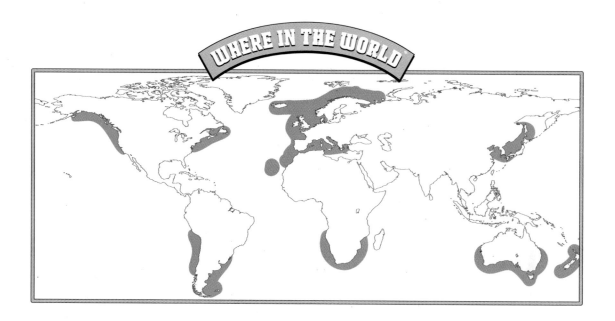

GREAT WHITE SHARK

STILL SWIMMING!

Great white sharks have been swimming the oceans for a long time!
Scientists believe they date back to the Paleocene epoch—
65 to 55 million years ago. This time period came immediately after
the mass extinction event of the Cretaceous era,
when the land dinosaurs died off.

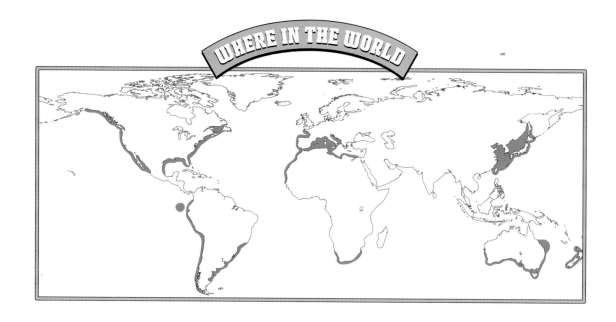

3D SHARKS
STICKER SHEET